French Phrases

FOR DUMMIES®

POCKET EDITION

**by Ed McCarthy and
Mary Ewing-Mulligan**

WILEY

Wiley Publishing, Inc.

French Wine For Dummies®, Pocket Edition

Published by
Wiley Publishing, Inc.
111 River Street
Hoboken, NJ 07030-5774
www.wiley.com

For general information on our other products and services, please contact our Customer Care Department within the U.S. at 800-762-2974, outside the U.S. at 317-572-3993, or fax 317-572-4002.

For technical support, please visit www.wiley.com/techsupport.

Wiley also publishes its books in a variety of electronic formats. Some content that appears in print may not be available in electronic books.

ISBN: 978-0-470-41429-3

Manufactured in the United States of America

10 9 8 7 6 5 4 3 2 1

Table of Contents

Introduction

●●●●●●●●●●●●●●●●●●●●●●●●●●●●

*W*e love French wines, and we want you to love them, too. We hope that by clearing away the confusion, we can incline you to experiment with French wines, so that you can discover a few types that you really enjoy.

We believe that wine drinkers like you can use *French Wine For Dummies,* Pocket Edition, for two reasons:

- ✔ French wines are a vast and confusing field — especially for people who don't speak French, who are accustomed to seeing wines named after grape varieties (which most French wines aren't). This book breaks down these barriers for you.

- ✔ The image of French wine is so prestigious that many people believe they need to know about France's wines, despite the difficulty inherent in mastering them. Having this book as your ally will give you confidence around French wines and eliminate whatever intimidation the wines' prestigious image might evoke.

Icons Used in This Book

 We're not trying to turn you into a winemaker or a French legislator, but some technical issues are important for understanding French wines — depending on how deeply you want to understand them, of course.

Advice and information that will make you a wiser French wine drinker and buyer is marked by this bull's-eye so that you won't miss it.

When you see this sign, you'll know that you're in the territory of a common misunderstanding about French wine. We alert you to help prevent confusion, or help you avoid a common mistake.

Some issues in wine are so fundamental that they bear repeating. Just so you don't think we repeated ourselves without realizing it, we'll mark the repetitions with this symbol.

Wine snobs practice all sorts of affectations designed to make other wine drinkers feel inferior. A comment such as "We *are* drinking classified growth Bordeaux tonight, aren't we?" can throw you for a loop. But you won't be intimidated by snobbery once you recognize it.

Where to Go from Here

You've got your minibook copy of *French Wine For Dummies,* Pocket Edition — now what? This minibook is a reference, so if you want to know more about Beaujolais Nouveau, head to Chapter 3. Or if you're interested in finding out more about elite Bordeaux, flip to Chapter 2. Or heck, start with Chapter 1 and read the chapters in order . . . you rebel. If you want even more advice about French wines, from the intricacies of wine laws and labels to the hidden gems of the Loire Valley, check out the full-size version of *French Wine For Dummies* — simply head to your local book seller or go to www.dummies.com.

Chapter 1
France, Superstar

Some people are just born with certain talents. Some countries are just born with certain gifts. In the case of France, the ability to grow wine grapes and make good wine is hard-wired into the land and the people who live there. That's why France is not only the greatest wine producing country on Earth, but also the greatest wine culture.

France has been the leader of the winemaking world for centuries. France is number one not only in wine production (in many years) but also in wine consumption. In the quality department, the most critically-acclaimed, most treasured red wines, white wines, sparkling wines, *and* sweet wines all come from France. The country's renown is such that winemakers from all over the world find inspiration and motivation in French wines.

In the Beginning . . .

The French have the Greeks and Romans to thank for getting them started as a wine producing land. As we remember so well from our Latin classes, Julius Caesar conquered Gaul in 51 B.C.; what the teacher didn't tell us, of course, was that the Roman troops almost certainly brought grapevine cuttings with them and planted them in what is now France.

The region of Provence, in southern France, was already a Roman province in the second century B.C. And long before that, in 600 B.C., the southern French city of Marseilles *(mar say)* was a Greek colony, most likely complete with vineyards.

By the 200s A.D., the areas known today as Bordeaux and Burgundy were producing wine, and by the 500s, grape growing and winemaking were common all over France.

Over the centuries, some wine regions of France became more important than others. Historically, the popularity of a region's wines had as much to do with politics and with proximity to waterways, for transportation of the wine, as it did with the quality of the wines themselves.

As one example, the wines of the Bordeaux region, in western France, benefited enormously from the fact that most of western France was part of England in the 12th century — making those wines less expensive to British wine drinkers than other French wines. That the city of Bordeaux is a major port didn't hurt, either. English demand spurred Bordeaux wine production in the 14th century, and Dutch enthusiasm for the wines helped bring Bordeaux to supremacy during the 17th and 18th centuries. Other wine regions of France progressed at a different pace, according to their own circumstances.

Everything hasn't necessarily been wine and roses for French winemakers, though. Three major fungal scourges (powdery mildew, downy mildew, and black rot) devastated their vineyards in the mid to late 19th century. And the phylloxera louse — an insect that eats vine roots — almost wiped out the entire species of wine grapes during the same period. But French wine rebounded. Today the wines of France are better than at any time in their history.

Natural Talents

France's thousands of years of winemaking experience count for a lot. But the fact is, France had a couple of other things going for her since Day One: climates extremely suitable for growing high quality wine grapes; and the right types of soils in the right climates.

France is large by European standards — it's the largest country in western Europe — but compared to countries such as the United States or Australia, it isn't really such a big place. (All of France could fit easily into Texas, for example, with plenty of room to spare.) And yet, France has a strong diversity of soil types and climates. Each of France's major wine regions has different growing conditions for its grapes. (Figure 1-1 depicts France's wine regions.)

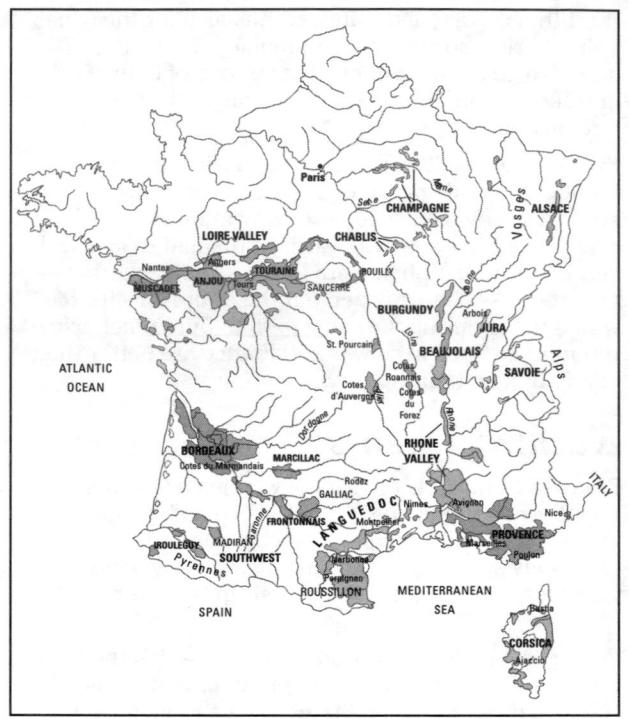

Figure 1-1: France's wine regions.

Climate ups and downs

 Because French wines are so acclaimed, wine people tend to credit France with having an ideal location for grape growing and winemaking. The 45th parallel, which runs through the regions of Bordeaux and the Rhône Valley, has taken on mythical connotations as the It position for fine wine production.

In reality, though, a lot of seriously good wine comes from places that occupy a much more southerly position than France does — such as all of Spain and Portugal, California, and most of Italy (not to mention, in the southern hemisphere, Chile, Argentina, Australia, New Zealand, and South Africa!). Furthermore, plenty of France's wine regions are even more northerly than Bordeaux; Champagne and Alsace, for example, are situated about as north as wine grapes can viably grow. From a global perspective, France would seem to be out of the mainstream of wine production, latitude-wise.

But latitude doesn't tell the whole story. France has ideal climates for growing wine grapes thanks to where the country happens to be situated relative to the rest of Europe, and thanks to the lay of the land within France's borders:

> ✔ Water surrounds France on three sides: the Atlantic Ocean on the west, the English Channel on the north, and the Mediterranean Sea along part of the country's southern border. These bodies of water influence the climate of the land nearby. In particular, winds passing over the Atlantic's Gulf Stream carry moisture and warm

air to western France, providing a climate that's more suitable for grape growing than France's northerly position might suggest.

✔ The Massif Central, a high plateau in south central France, blocks the Atlantic's maritime influence about halfway across the country — and creates a particular climate in eastern France (hot but relatively short summers, and cold winters) that's distinctly different from the damp, temperate climate in the west. Farther east, France is landlocked and mountainous, with the mighty Alps Mountains separating France from Italy and Switzerland.

✔ The Mediterranean Sea creates yet another climate pattern in southern France: warm, dry, long summers and mild, rainy winters.

 According to the way experts categorize climates, in fact, France boasts all three of the major climates for grape growing and wine production:

✔ The maritime climate (in the Bordeaux region and elsewhere in western France)

✔ The continental climate (in the regions of Alsace and Burgundy)

✔ The Mediterranean climate (in the southern Rhône Valley region and in southern France)

These different climates each favor the cultivation of different grape varieties and the production of different types of wine.

Old dirt

The variation in soil types within France has to do with the geological origins of the European continent — the melting of polar ice caps, the drying of seas, the decomposition of rocks, and so forth. We know of two books devoted entirely to the subsoils and the soils of France's wine regions: that's how complex the soils are.

Different wine regions of France have markedly different soils; for example:

- ✔ Gravel in the western part of Bordeaux
- ✔ Chalky soil in Champagne, in the northeast
- ✔ Granite in Beaujolais, in the southeast
- ✔ Large stones in the Châteauneuf-du-Pape district of the southern Rhône Valley

And even within individual wine regions, the soil varies quite a lot. The difference between western Bordeaux and eastern Bordeaux is one classic example: different soils in each area favor different grape varieties. Within the region of Alsace, the soils change literally from one hillside to the next, and within Burgundy, soils change between vineyards separated from each other by the width of a cow path.

None of this is to say that French dirt is any better than any other country's dirt, though. What's important about France's soils is that they are the right soils in the right climates for the right grape varieties. Where the climate is rainy (as in Bordeaux), for example, the soil provides good drainage. Where there's an impressionable grape variety, such as Pinot Noir, the soil varies from patch to patch (as in Burgundy) to create compellingly individual wines. And so forth.

French Wine-Think

We picture the French as sensualists, romantics, and lovers. When it comes to wine, they're also quite humble. Sure, most Frenchman believe that French wines are the greatest wines anywhere — but they don't take personal credit for that greatness.

The French believe that their wines are so exceptional because their land is blessed. They attribute every nuance in a wine to the particular place where the grapes grow — to the rain that falls or refrains from falling; the sun that shines down on the vineyard; the wind that warms or cools the air; and the soil that holds the rain or drains it, that reflects the sun's heat back onto the grapes, or contains just the right minerals.

The French have a single word for the whole package of natural, interactive forces that affect the grapevine and its fruit: *terroir* (pronounced *ter wahr*). *Terroir* encompasses:

- ✔ The soil and subsoil of a vineyard, including its mineral content, fertility, and drainage

- ✔ How the vineyard is situated, on a slope, for example, or near a river

- ✔ The climate of the wine region, including sun, heat, wind, rain, and humidity

- ✔ The grape variety or varieties that grow in the vineyard

Every wine comes from a unique *terroir,* and — in the Gallic way of looking at wine — is what it is because of its *terroir.*

Of course, every French wine also has a winemaker who turns the fruit of the vineyard into wine. And there's no arguing with the fact that what the winemaker does — such as fermenting the grape juice at a certain temperature or aging a wine in a particular type of oak barrel — can affect the quality and style of the wine. For the most part, however, French winemakers perceive their responsibility as bringing out in the wine what the *terroir* put into the grapes. (And because of the long history of each region, the winemakers have a pretty good idea of what that is.)

The title that most French winemakers use — *vigneron* — suggests what they consider their role to be. The word means winegrower, not winemaker. Their wines grow from their vineyards, rather than being "made" in their wineries.

The concept of *terroir* is so fundamental to French wine that it even dictates how the wines are named: The overwhelming majority of French wines carry the name of the place where the grapes grow, because the place (rather than just the grape variety) is what makes the wines the way they are. Depending on the wine, the place might be any of the following:

- ✔ A large wine region
- ✔ A district within a region
- ✔ Even a single vineyard

A Note on Names

If a wine comes from a classic region, the label will carry the words "*Appellation . . . Contrôlée*" (*ahp pel laht zee ohn con troh lay*) in small print under the name of the wine. Between the two words is the name of the place that's the wine official name.

Appellation Contrôlée translates as "regulated name." Sometimes, in reading about French wines, you might see the phrase *Appellation d'Origine Contrôlée;* it translates as "regulated place name." The two phrases are used interchangeably and mean the same thing. People who talk about wine a lot use the abbreviations "AC" or "AOC" for these phrases.

Chapter 2
Elite Red Wines of Bordeaux

● ●

In This Chapter

► Why Bordeaux sets the standard

► Left Bank-Right Bank styles

► Bordeaux's upper crust wines

► When to drink red Bordeaux

● ●

*B*efore we ever tasted our first Bordeaux wine (many years ago — don't ask how many), we knew that Bordeaux wines must be special, because whenever anyone uttered the word "Bordeaux," it was with a tone of awe and respect. At first, we found Bordeaux confusing, what with all its districts, sub-districts, and villages — not to mention the classifications of specific properties, and the different types of classifications in different districts! But gradually, we figured it all out.

Now, thousands of Bordeaux wines later, we're the ones holding Bordeaux in awe. The wines meet the test of time for us. Of all the different kinds of wines we've enjoyed, the largest percentage of truly great wines have been red Bordeaux wines. Hands down. No contest. Yes, there is something special about Bordeaux.

The Bordeaux Advantage

The Bordeaux wine region lies in the southern part of western France, on the Atlantic coast (see Figure 1-1). The Gironde Estuary and its two major rivers, the Dordogne and the Garonne, run through the heart of the region. Almost all of Bordeaux's great wine estates are near the Gironde or one of its tributaries. The city of Bordeaux, France's fourth largest city, lies in the center of the region.

The Bordeaux area has a maritime climate, with damp springtimes, rather hot, fairly dry summers, rather mild winters, and quite a bit of rain during autumn and winter. When rain does occur in the fall, it often spells trouble for the vintage: Too much rain can turn a promising grape crop into a mediocre one.

Bordeaux's superiority derives from the region's very special *terroir,* its unique combination of climate and soil. It's also due to the fact that, throughout the centuries, the Bordelais have figured out which grape varieties grow best in their locale. And that the varieties that thrive there happen to be among the greatest varieties in the world.

Bordeaux the red

Bordeaux's reputation as a great wine region rests on its most superb reds, legendary and long-lived wines made by historic wine estates (called *châteaux*), which can improve for several decades. Seventy-five to 80 percent of Bordeaux's wines are red. (Most of the rest is dry white, and 2 or 3 percent is stunning dessert wine.)

The greatest, most age-worthy red Bordeaux wines start at $30 a bottle retail, and can go up to about $800 a bottle and more for rare wines such as a newly-released Château Pétrus — with older, fine vintages of the greatest and rarest wines even more expensive. But the famous, costly wines make up only about 2 to 3 percent of all red Bordeaux.

Red Bordeaux's grape varieties

Red Bordeaux is always a blended wine. It's made from two to five so-called *black* grape varieties. The percentage of each grape variety used in a particular red Bordeaux wine can change from year to year, depending on the climate, and how each variety has fared during the growing season. The percentage also varies from one estate to another.

The five grape varieties of red Bordeaux are the following:

- ✔ Cabernet Sauvignon *(cab er nay so vee n'yohn)*
- ✔ Merlot *(mer loh)*
- ✔ Cabernet Franc *(cab er nay frahn)*
- ✔ Petit Verdot *(peh tee vair doe)*
- ✔ Malbec *(mahl bec)*

Either Cabernet Sauvignon or Merlot is the dominant variety in practically all red Bordeaux wines; Cabernet Franc is the third most-utilized variety, followed by Petite Verdot and Malbec.

The High-Rent Districts

The Bordeaux region is quite large, encompassing more than a quarter of a million acres of vineyards, and it produces about 660 million bottles annually (about 10 percent of France's wine, but more than 25 percent of its AOC wine). Naturally, climate and soil vary across this large area. Four major districts, each with its own particular *terroir,* exist within the region:

- **Haut-Médoc** *(oh meh dock)*
- **Graves/Pessac-Léognan** *(grahv/peh sack lay oh nyahn)*
- **St.-Emilion** *(sant em eel yon)*
- **Pomerol** *(pohm eh roll)*

Wines with the Haut-Médoc, St.-Emilion, or Pomerol appellations must be red; Graves or Pessac-Léognan wines may be red or white.

Because of certain similarities in the wines, and for historical reasons, these four major districts for red Bordeaux are often grouped as two entities, which are often known as the *Left Bank* and the *Right Bank.* The Médoc peninsula and Graves/Pessac-Léognan make up the Left Bank and St.-Emilion and Pomerol are Right Bank districts.

The Left Bank style

Our own very favorite red Bordeaux wines come from the Left Bank of Bordeaux, especially from the Haut-Médoc and Pessac-Léognan.

The soil on the Left Bank is primarily gravelly, with excellent drainage. Although the area is relatively flat, mounds or terraces of gravel, left by a retreating sea thousands of years ago, exist throughout the Left Bank. Cabernet Sauvignon, which does very well in gravelly soil, is the predominant red grape variety of the Left Bank. A typical Bordeaux from the Haut-Médoc or

Pessac-Léognan usually has 60 to 65 percent Cabernet Sauvignon in its blend, with about 25 to 30 percent Merlot.

Generally speaking, the red Bordeaux wines from the Left Bank are quite tannic and austere when they are young (see *Wine For Dummies,* 4th Edition, published by Wiley, for an explanation of "tannic"), and they have a pronounced black currant aroma and flavor. With age, they develop complex secondary aromas and flavors, such as stewed fruit, leather, earth, and tobacco; their colors lighten and flavors soften, as the tannin begins to drop out of the wine.

 These wines need ten years or more to come into their own, and the best of them are capable of developing further for decades. The most common mistake regarding Left Bank Bordeaux wines is drinking them when they're less than ten years old: They can taste harsh and bitter at this age, and then you wonder what all the fuss is about red Bordeaux.

The Villages of the Haut-Médoc

Of the four major districts in Bordeaux, the Haut-Médoc historically has been the most important one during the last two centuries. It is here that many of the most famous Bordeaux wines are made.

The Haut-Médoc encompasses four villages that rank among the aristocracy of wine names. Each of the four major communes produces wines of a distinct style, which experienced tasters can identify without knowing the wine's provenance. Table 2-1 describes the different characteristics of the four major communes' wines.

Table 2-1	The Haut-Médoc's Big Four Wine Villages
Village	**Typical Style of Its Wines**
Margaux	Fragrant aroma; elegant, medium-bodied, supple wines with complex flavors; a typical Margaux wine is Château Palmer. Also home to Château Margaux, one of Bordeaux's most famous wines.
St.-Julien	Flavorful, rich, medium- to full-bodied wines; subtle, balanced, and consistent; a typical St.-Julien wine is Château Ducru-Beaucaillou.
Pauillac	Black currant and cedar aromas; powerful, firm, rich, tannic, full-bodied, concentrated wines that are very long-lived; home of three famous Bordeaux: Châteaux Lafite-Rothschild, Latour, and Mouton-Rothschild; a typical Pauillac wine is Château Pichon-Lalande.
St.-Estèphe	Dark-colored, austere, full-bodied, tannic, acidic, earthy wines; very long-lived, needing time to evolve; a typical St.-Estèphe wine is Château Montrose.

The names of these villages are an official part of the names of the wines made within these communes. Any wines from the Haut-Médoc which do not come from vineyards within these communes carry the broader appellation, "Appellation Haut-Médoc Contrôlée."

The Right Bank style

The Right Bank, with its two major sub-regions of St.-Emilion and Pomerol has soil that tends to be a mixture of clay, silt, sand, and limestone. In this *terroir,* the Merlot grape variety flourishes and is clearly the Right

Bank's dominant grape variety. Cabernet Franc, which ripens faster than Cabernet Sauvignon, is the second-most important variety on the Right Bank.

Right Bank Bordeaux reds, such as St.-Emilions and Pomerols, are a good choice for the novice red Bordeaux drinker because they are less tannic and austere, and more approachable, than Left Bank Bordeaux. This difference is particularly noticeable when the wines are young (less than ten years old).

Although Right Bank red Bordeaux wines are readier to drink sooner than Left Bank Bordeaux, the better examples of these wines can live for many decades — nearly as long as Left Bank Bordeaux, especially in good vintages.

 Generally speaking, the wines of Pomerol are the most expensive Bordeaux wines and the most difficult to find — for the simple reason that these wines come from the smallest wine estates of any of the major Bordeaux sub-regions. For instance, the typical Haut-Médoc wine estate produces about 20,000 to 25,000 cases (12 bottles to a case) of wine annually, while the average Pomerol winery makes only 3,000 to 5,000 cases of wine a year.

Classified Information

Because so many Bordeaux wines are so renowned, down through the years many people have attempted to rank them, according to the wines' merit or quality. These rankings, or classifications, have become an important part of the region's lore.

The 1855 Classification

No classification of Bordeaux wines has created more of an impact than the "1855 Classification of the Great Growths of the Gironde." Here's how this legendary classification came about.

The 1855 Exposition in Paris was going to have a special guest — Queen Victoria of England. Since the Brits had always been partial to Bordeaux (and, in fact, owned this region at one time, then called Aquitaine), the organizers of the Exposition asked the Bordeaux Chamber of Commerce to develop the ultimate classification of great Bordeaux wines. The Chamber of Commerce in turn asked the *négociants* of Bordeaux — the merchants who bought and sold Bordeaux wine — to devise the list. The *négociants* based their classification on the prices that the wines commanded at that time, as well as the wines' track records over the past 100 years, and came up with a ranked list of 61 red Bordeaux wines.

These 61 wines became known as "Classified Growths" or, in French, *"Grands Crus Classés"* wines (a *cru* in Bordeaux refers to a wine estate). At that time, the Haut-Médoc sub-region dominated the Bordeaux wine trade, and so 60 of the 61 wines were Haut-Médoc wines; one was from the Graves (the part now known as Pessac-Léognan). All of the Right Bank wines were shut out of the famous 1855 ranking.

The 1855 Classification divided the 61 classified growths into five categories, or classes, according to quality. The top five of the list, or "first growths," are

- ✔ **Château Lafite-Rothschild**
- ✔ **Château Latour**
- ✔ **Château Margaux**
- ✔ **Château Haut Brion** (Graves)
- ✔ **Château Mouton-Rothschild** (elevated from a Second Growth in 1973)

Other classifications

Two other classifications are the Graves/Pessac-Léognan and the St.-Emilion classifications.

In 1953, the Graves/Pessac-Léognan officially rated the red wines and the dry white wines of the Graves. The 1953 classification named 13 red Graves wines (all in what is now the Pessac-Léognan district), but did not rank them individually. All the area's top estates — such as Château Haut Brion, Château La Mission-Brion, Domaine de Chevalier, and Château Pape Clément — are classified growths, or *Crus Classés*.

The St.-Emilion classification, in 1955, first rated the reds of this region and provides for revisions every decade. Currently, 13 wines hold the highest St.-Emilion ranking, "Premier Grand Cru Classé." The two highest are

- ✔ **Château Ausone**
- ✔ **Château Cheval Blanc**

Experiencing a great, mature Bordeaux

Red Bordeaux wines go through a complete metamorphosis as they age. When they're young, they usually have deep cranberry color — some darker than others, depending on the wine and the vintage. They have all sorts of aromas, which could include black currants, spices, plums, cassis, and cedar. They are very dry in this youthful stage, and the tannins in the wine can sometimes mask the fruit flavors.

When red Bordeaux ages, the color turns garnet, first at its edge, and then throughout the wine. With more age, as the wine's tannin literally drops out as sediment, the color becomes distinctly lighter, taking on a light brownish-red hue. The wine develops a more complex bouquet and flavor, sometimes with hints of leather, tobacco, and/or stewed fruit. The wine tastes softer and sweeter, with a wonderful, lingering aftertaste. You are now tasting a mature Bordeaux — one of the great gustatory experiences. A hunk of hard cheese, such as Cheddar or Asiago, and some crusty bread, and you're all set!

Bordeaux's Best Reds

Sorry, we can't keep our spoons out of the soup. Even after all the official classifications, we still feel the need to give you our own personal list of the very best Bordeaux wines today.

Our top ten

Ten wines occupy our elite class of red Bordeaux. They include the five First Growths, one "super second" growth (all from the famous 1855 Classification), the two best St.-Emilion wines, and the two best Pomerols. We do not attempt to list these wines in any particular order of preference; they're all great, and each Bordeaux lover has his or her own favorites.

First Growth

Château Lafite-Rothschild (Pauillac, Haut-Médoc)

Château Latour (Pauillac, Haut-Médoc)

Château Margaux (Margaux, Haut-Médoc)

Château Haut Brion (Pessac-Léognan)

Château Mouton-Rothschild (Pauillac, Haut-Médoc)

Second Growth

Château Léoville-Las Cases, (St.-Julien, Haut-Médoc)

St.-Emilion

Château Ausone

Château Cheval Blanc

Pomerol

Château Pétrus

Château Lafleur

Unfortunately, all ten of these wines are very expensive, and a few (Ausone, Pétrus, and Lafleur) are very difficult to find. But since Bordeaux is a huge wine region, it offers scores of other great wines nearly as fine and considerably less costly than these ten elite wines. In the next sections, we list some of the best red Bordeaux wines on the Left and Right Banks.

Great Haut-Médoc wines

Our favorite Haut-Médoc wines (after those named among our Top Ten) are all classified growths. We list them in our rough order of preference and include their village appellation after the wine.

Château Pichon-Longueville — Comtesse de Lalande, Pauillac

Château Ducru-Beaucaillou, Saint-Julien

Château Palmer, Margaux

Château Pichon-Longueville Baron, Pauillac

Château Gruaud-Larose, St.-Julien

Château Montrose, St.-Estèphe

Château Clerc-Milon, Pauillac

Château Grand-Puy-Lacoste, Pauillac

Château Léoville-Barton, St.-Julien

Château Lynch-Bages, Pauillac

Top Pessac-Léognan wines

 Most of our favorite Pessac-Léognan wines are classified growths (in 1953 and 1959); only three of them are unclassified. Château Haut-Brion, which makes our Top Ten, isn't repeated here. We list them in our rough order of preference:

Château La Mission-Haut-Brion

Château Pape-Clément

Château Malartic-Lagravière

Château Smith-Haut-Lafitte

Domaine de Chevalier

Château Les Carmes Haut-Brion (unclassified)

Château La Tour-Haut-Brion

Château Larrivet–Haut-Brion (unclassified)

Château La Louvière (unclassified)

Château d'Olivier

The Best St.-Emilion Bordeaux

The two greatest St.-Emilion wines, Château Cheval Blanc and Château Ausone, are among our Top Ten elite wines mentioned earlier in this chapter. Otherwise, we list our favorites in our rough order of preference, and mention their official classification rank.

Château Pavie (Premier Grand Cru Classé)

Château Pavie-Macquin (Grand Cru Classé)

Château Canon-La-Gaffelière (Grand Cru Classé)

Château Pavie-Decesse (Grand Cru Classé)

Château Troplong-Mondot (Grand Cru Classé)

Château Beau-Séjour Bécot (Premier Grand Cru Classé)

Château Monbousquet (Grand Cru)

Château La Clusière (Grand Cru Classé)

Clos de l'Oratoire (Grand Cru Classé)

Château Figeac (Premier Grand Cru Classé)

A Pomerol ranking (unofficial)

Even though the wines of the Pomerol sub-region — which, like St.-Emilion's, are all red — have never been officially classified, we've come up with our own ranking of these very wonderful wines. We list the wines in our rough order of preference.

Château Pétrus

Château Lafleur

Château Trotanoy

Château L'Evangile

Vieux-Château-Certan

Château L'Eglise-Clinet

Château Clinet

Château La Fleur Pétrus

Clos L'Eglise

Château La Conseillante

Drinking Red Bordeaux

We seldom order the best red Bordeaux wines in restaurants because the young wines from the currently available vintages that dominate wine lists are far from ready to drink. And when older vintages *are* available, their prices are usually very expensive. The best restaurant strategy is to drink inexpensive, readier-to-drink red Bordeaux — if they are available. Save the better, mature red Bordeaux for drinking at home or at your friends' homes.

Red Bordeaux is not the easiest wine to match with food. It goes best with simple cuts of red meat, lamb, or venison. It's also fine with hard cheeses, such as Cheddar or Comté, and good, crusty bread.

A fine Bordeaux needs decanting, whether it's young or mature. A young wine will benefit from the extra aeration (at least an hour) that decanting provides. A mature (ten years or older) Bordeaux has sediment, a harmless but disagreeable by-product, that's removed by careful decanting. Inexpensive Bordeaux wines do not need decanting.

Serve red Bordeaux at cool room temperatures — about 63°F to 66°F (18° to 19°C). A fine, large glass (not too wide) is best.

Chapter 3
Burgundy and Beaujolais

A legend about French red wine is that Burgundy seduces you when you're young, with all her voluptuous charms, but you grow into the safer, surer wines of Bordeaux with age. But many swear Burgundy is the best red in the world and remain devoted to Burgundy for life.

Beaujolais, on the other hand, is unabashedly the fun red. The Beaujolais region is unique among French wine regions because it makes wines that are happy to please without trying to impress. Some Beaujolais wines are better than others, sure — but even the best wines, such as a good Moulin-à-Vent, don't require con- templative attention.

The Where and Why of Burgundy

Burgundy is a long, narrow wine region in eastern France, southeast of Paris (see Figure 1-1). The French call the region *Bourgogne,* pronounced *bor guh nyeh*.

Burgundy is a slightly fragmented region, consisting of four somewhat contiguous districts and one district that's about 70 miles northwest of the rest of the region. Because of its unique *terroir* — the special growing conditions in the vineyards — the Burgundy region excels in both white and red wines.

Soil and climate

The soils of Burgundy are extremely varied, in their richness, depth, and mineral content. Most vineyards have a base soil of limestone overlaid with limestone and marl (a mixture of clay and limestone), sometimes mixed with sand or gravel. Where limestone is dominant, white wines grow; where more marl exists, grapes for red wine grow.

The climate in Burgundy is continental for the most part: fairly warm summers, with the constant threat of hail, and cold winters. The region is northerly enough and cool enough that the grapes just about ripen in most years. Not every year is a good vintage; some years bring too much rain, or are too cool.

The two great Burgundy grapes

Nearly all the red wines of the Burgundy region derive from Pinot Noir. Pinot Noir is notorious throughout the wine world for being difficult to cultivate because it requires very specific soil and climate parameters to produce its best fruit. Burgundy has that climate and soil.

Chardonnay is the other important variety in the Burgundy region and the basis for the region's most important white wines. Although Chardonnay is a nearly universal variety today, it reaches its height in Burgundy, where it makes complex, masterful wines that can age for decades.

The scale of Burgundy

Burgundy is a region of small vineyards, mixed ownership of vineyards, and relatively small production. Excluding the Beaujolais district, Burgundy produces a total of about 22 million cases of wine annually. (Beaujolais is technically part of Burgundy, but really a separate type of wine — see later in the chapter.) This quantity is only about a small part of Bordeaux's production.

Burgundy's vineyards are also much smaller than Bordeaux's, meaning that less wine is available from any one vineyard. Where large vineyards do exist in Burgundy, they have multiple owners, so that many different wines exist from that one vineyard.

The limited scale of production in Burgundy has three repercussions:

- ✔ The wines are expensive because production is small.

- ✔ Multiple brands of any one wine are available.

> ✔ The name of a vineyard is not a reliable indication
> of a wine's quality, because every vineyard has
> several owners and winemakers, who vary in dedi-
> cation and ability.

If Burgundy is beginning to sound like a labyrinth to
you — well, you've grasped the true complexity of the
region. But like anything worth having, the reward of a
fabulous Burgundy is worth the effort.

Burgundy's AOC System

Because Burgundy is one of France's classic wine
regions, the vast majority of wines produced there are
AOC wines. (For more information on France's AOC
system of naming and defining wines, turn to Chapter 1.)

Burgundy's AOCs fall into four categories, according to
the nature of their territory. From the most general to
the most specific (and prestigious), these categories
are the following:

> ✔ **Region-wide appellations:** The grapes for these
> wines can grow throughout the Burgundy region.

> ✔ **District-specific appellations:** These wines come
> from grapes grown in a single district of Burgundy,
> or part of a district. We name the various districts
> of Burgundy in the next section.

> ✔ **Village-specific appellations:** The grapes for these
> wines can grow only in the territory of certain vil-
> lages (also called *communes,* or communities) that
> are named in the AOC regulations.

✔ **Vineyard-specific appellations:** The grapes for
each of these wines must come from a single vineyard that is recognized in the AOC regulations.
Vineyards are divided into two levels: *Premier cru*
vineyards and *Grand cru* vineyards.

Burgundy's Districts

Burgundy is a complex (and, some might say, compli-
cated) region that encompasses four distinct wine districts. From north to south, they are Chablis, Côte d'Or,
Côte Chalonnaise, and Mâconnais.

Chablis, from Chablis, France

The Chablis district, the northernmost outpost of
Burgundy, produces white wines only, 100 percent
Chardonnay. Chablis's climate is generally cool, similar
to that of the Champagne region to its north.

In a good vintage, Chablis can be magical: pale straw in
color with hints of green, turning light gold with age;
bone dry and medium-bodied, with lively acidity that
makes the wine great with seafood; concentrated in
delicate, minerally aromas and an appley flavor that
lingers long after you swallow.

The soil in the Chablis area, which undoubtedly contributes to the wine's minerally qualities, has lots of
limestone and chalky clay, of a type called Kimmeridgian
clay; this soil contains fragments of billions of fossilized
oyster shells, deposited by the sea which once covered
Chablis. Is this the reason that Chablis goes so well with
oysters? Probably so.

Producers make Chablis in three different styles:

✔ Many use just stainless steel tanks, with absolutely no oak barrels at all — either in fermenting or aging the wine — in order to preserve the purest expression of Chablis's flavors; the producer Louis Michel is the greatest proponent of this style; other "no oak" producers include Jean-Marc Brocard, Long-Depaquit, A. Régnard, and Jean Durup.

✔ A few producers ferment or briefly age their wines in oak barrels, mainly used barrels that give less oaky flavor than new barrels; this style of Chablis is typically more full-bodied and can have some oaky aroma and flavor; Raveneau and René & Vincent Dauvissat are the leading producers of this style of Chablis.

✔ Quite a few producers are taking the middle ground, using no oak for their less-expensive Chablis, and some oak aging for their more serious wines; these producers include Collet, Jean-Paul Droin, Jean Dauvissat, William Fèvre, and Domaine Laroche.

 You can find good Chablis producers in all three styles. Our favorite Chablis producers, in our rough order of preference, are the following (the first three are virtually tied for first):

François & Jean-Marie Raveneau

René & Vincent Dauvissat

Louis Michel & Fils

Jean Collet

Jean-Paul Droin

Jean Dauvissat

Verget

Gérard Duplessis

William Fèvre

Christian Moreau Père et Fils

Domaine Laroche

Long-Depaquit

Jean-Claude Bessin

Billaud-Simon

Burgundy Royalty: Côte d'Or

Most wine lovers associate the word "Burgundy" specifically with the wines from the Côte d'Or, the heart of the Burgundy region. The Côte d'Or produces all levels of Burgundy wine. District-level appellations that you might occasionally see on wine labels include Côte de Nuits-Villages, Côte de Beaune-Villages, Hautes-Côtes-de-Nuits, and Hautes-Côtes-de-Beaune.

The reds and whites of the Côte d'Or are the best that Burgundy has to offer — and they are priced accordingly.

 So that you can spend your Burgundy dollars wisely, we recommend that you follow the following criteria, listed in order of importance, when choosing your red or white Burgundy wines:

✔ **The producer's reputation:** Consult recent newsletters, review the list in the next section of this book, or ask a knowledgeable wine merchant.

✔ **The vintage:** The Burgundy region experiences considerable variation in quality and style from year to year.

✔ **The appellation:** The name of the commune and/or the vineyard, although significant, is invariably less important than the producer or the vintage.

Our top 10 Côte d'Or Red Burgundy producers (in our rough order of preference) are the following:

Domaine (and Maison) Leroy

Domaine de la Romanée-Conti

Domaine du Comte de Vogüé

Domaine Anne Gros

Domaine Hubert Lignier

Domaine Claude Dugat

Domaine Robert Groffier

Clos de Tart

Domaine Joseph Roty

Domaine Jean Grivot

A few of the outstanding Côte d'Or White Burgundy producers (listed in alphabetical order) include the following:

Domaine Louis Carillon & Fils

Domaine Jean-François Coche-Dury

Domaine des Comtes Lafon

Domaine Leflaive

Domaine Ramonet

Domaine Étienne Sauzet

The Côte Chalonnaise: affordable Burgundies

The Côte Chalonnaise district boasts five wine villages that are good sources of very decent, affordable red and white Burgundies. Côte Chalonnaise Burgundies aren't quite so fine as most Côte d'Or Burgundies; they tend to be a bit earthier and have less complex aromas and flavors. But they are good values, and they are excellent choices in restaurants or for everyday drinking.

We recommend the following producers of Côte Chalonnaise wines (listed in alphabetical order):

Domaine Bertrand (Montagny)

René Bourgeon (Givry Blanc)

Domaine Jean-Claude Brelière (Rully)

Domaine Michel Briday (Rully)

Château de Chamirey (Antonin Rodet — Mercurey Rouge and Blanc)

Château de Rully (Antonin Rodet — both Rully Blanc and Rouge)

J. Faiveley (Mercurey Rouge and Blanc; Rully Blanc; Montagny)

Château Genot-Boulanger (Mercurey)

Domaine Joblot (Givry)

Domaine Michel Juillot (Mercurey Rouge and Blanc)

Olivier Leflaive Frères (Rully Blanc; Mercurey Blanc)

Domaine Thierry Lespinasse (Givry)

Domaine de la Rénarde (Rully)

Everyday whites: the Mâcon

The city of Mâcon *(mah cawn)* is located at the southern end of the Mâconnais — a wine district directly south of the Côte Chalonnaise, and north of Beaujolais. As you travel into the Mâconnais, the weather becomes warmer and sunnier, more and more Mediterranean. Almost all of the Mâcon wine that's exported is white.

The wines of Mâcon and Mâcon-Villages *(mac cawn vee lahj)* are medium-bodied, fresh, crisp, lively, and almost always made without the use of oak. Drink them when they are young — within three years of the vintage.

The most famous Mâcon wine is undoubtedly Pouilly-Fuissé *(poo yee fwee say)*, the most full-bodied and the most expensive wine of the Mâconnais. Pouilly-Fuissé wines come from a vineyard area around the villages of Pouilly and Fuissé, and, unlike simpler Mâcon white wines, are usually aged in small oak barrels.

 St.-Véran *(san veh rahn)* wines have about half the production (250,000 cases annually) of Pouilly-Fuissé, and are far better values. These wines are similar to Pouilly-Fuissé, but are less full-bodied.

The following are our recommended producers of Mâcon, Mâcon-Villages, Viré-Clessé, and St.-Véran wines, listed in our rough order of preference:

Verget	Louis Jadot
Domaine Jean Thévenet	Joseph Drouhin
Domaine Valette	Manciat-Poncet
Jean-Claude Thévenet	André Bonhomme
Roger Lasserat	Emilian Gillet
Louis Latour	Olivier Merlin

The following are our recommended producers of Pouilly-Fuissé wines, listed in our rough order of preference:

M. Vincent /Château Fuisse	Domaine Valette
Daniel Barraud	Manciat-Poncet
Domaine J.A. Ferrat	Thierry Guérin
Domaine Robert Denogent	Château de Beauregard
Verget	Roger Lasserat
	Louis Latour
	Louis Jadot

Serving Burgundy

Unlike red Bordeaux, red Burgundy from the Côte d'Or can be consumed when it's relatively young, after five or six years. The reason is that the Pinot Noir grape contains far less tannin than Cabernet Sauvignon or Merlot — Bordeaux's grape varieties.

Serve your red Burgundies slightly cool — about 60° to 62° F (17° C) in a fine, wide-bowled glass. Do *not* decant red Burgundies; pour them straight from the bottle. Too much aeration causes you to lose some of your wine's wonderful aromas — one of its greatest qualities.

White Côte d'Or Burgundies are among the most long-lived white wines in the world. In good vintages, the best white Burgundies, such as Corton-Charlemagne or a *grand cru* Montrachet, can age for 20 years or more. Unlike red Burgundies, the better whites need time, often ten years or more, to really develop and open up. We recommend that you *do decant your serious white Burgundies;* they truly benefit from the extra aeration.

Serve fine white Burgundies slightly cooler than red — about 55° to 58° F (13° to 15° C). You can't appreciate their wonderful, complex flavors when they are too cold. We enjoy our good white Burgundies in a wide-bowled glass, just slightly smaller than the glass we use for red Burgundies.

Beaujolais, The Fun Red

Administratively, Beaujolais is a district of the Burgundy region, but the red wine of Beaujolais is so different from those in the rest of Burgundy — made from a different grape variety grown in different soil and a warmer climate — that we consider Beaujolais to be a wine region in its own right, distinct from Burgundy.

The Beaujolais terroir

Beaujolais is near enough to the Mediterranean Sea to experience Mediterranean-like summer weather, which is warm and dry; but the region is also interior enough to experience cold, dry weather from the northeast, including spring frosts. Overall, the climate is temperate.

Soil variations are the most significant factor in defining the character of the region's various wines:

- ✔ In the southern part of the region, south of the town of Villefranche, the soils are sandstone or clay and limestone.

- ✔ In the north, the soils are granite or schist (crystalline rock) on the upper slopes, with stone and clay soils on the lower slopes.

Just as the soils are different in the north, so are the wines. The sturdiest, firmest Beaujolais wines come from the northern vineyards, while the lightest, most supple wines come from southern vineyards.

The Gamay grape

Except for a small amount of Chardonnay, 99 percent of the Beaujolais vineyards are covered by a single grape variety, Gamay; all red Beaujolais wine derives entirely from Gamay.

Gamay exists in a few other places — France's Loire Valley, for example, and Switzerland — but the Beaujolais region is truly the stronghold for this variety, and the finest Gamay wines come from this area. (Neither the grape called Gamay Beaujolais in California nor the grape called Napa Gamay is true Gamay.)

The Gamay variety makes wines that are fairly deep in color, with a bluish tinge. They tend to have light to medium body, relatively low acidity, moderate tannin, and aromas and flavors of red berries.

From Frivolous to Firm

Not all Beaujolais wine is the same. Soil differences throughout the region and subtle variations in winemaking technique cause the wines to vary considerably in style — from light-bodied, precocious wines at one end of the spectrum to denser, fuller-bodied wines at the other end. All these wines are dry.

Beaujolais and Beaujolais-Villages

The lightest wines, from the southern part of the region, usually carry the region's most basic appellation, "Beaujolais." These wines are generally light-bodied with low tannin and pronounced, youthful fruity aromas and flavors; they are wines to drink young, in the first year after the harvest. Wines with the appellation Beaujolais Supérieur are basic Beaujolais wines that have a higher minimum alcohol content.

A separate type of Beaujolais comes from grapes grown in the territory of 39 villages in the northern part of the region: "Beaujolais-Villages" *(bo jho lay vee lahj)*. These wines are fuller and more substantial than simple Beaujolais wines, thanks to the schist and granite soils of the north — but they are still fruity, fresh, youthful wines for consuming young, until they are about two years old. Beaujolais-Villages wines account for 25 percent of all Beaujolais production.

Beaujolais Nouveau

Beaujolais Nouveau, *new Beaujolais,* is the lightest, fruitiest, most exuberant style of Beaujolais. It differs from other Beaujolais wines not according to where it comes from, but according to how it's made: with minimum aging and maximum personality. Beaujolais Nouveau is designed to be delicious when it is barely two months old.

Beaujolais Nouveau is the first French wine to be released from each year's new crop of grapes. By mid-November, the wine is already bottled and on its way to market. On the third Thursday of November the wine becomes legal: Wine drinkers all over the world open bottles to celebrate the harvest.

Cru Beaujolais

The best Beaujolais wines come from ten specific zones in the north. They carry the name of the area where the grapes grow; their official appellations don't use the word "Beaujolais" at all. (Many labels for the U.S. market do carry the words "Red Beaujolais Wine" in small print, however.)

The wines from these ten areas are known as *cru Beaujolais*. *Cru* Beaujolais wines are firmer, richer and more refined than other Beaujolais wines. But generalizations about these wines are problematic, because the *cru* wines vary in style from one *cru* to another.

The ten *cru* Beaujolais, from south to north, are:

- **Brouilly** *(broo yee)*
- **Côte de Brouilly**
- **Régnié** *(ray nyay)*
- **Morgon** *(mor gohn)*
- **Chiroubles** *(sheh roob leh)*
- **Fleurie** *(flehr ee)*
- **Moulin-à-Vent** *(moo lahn ah vahn)*
- **Chénas** *(shay nahs)*
- **Juliénas** *(jool yay nahs)*
- **St.-Amour** *(sant ah more)*

Enjoying Beaujolais

Beaujolais is best when it's young, because with age it loses its distinctiveness. The lighter the style, the younger the wine should be. Here are some general guidelines:

- **Beaujolais Nouveau:** Drink as young as possible; it will still be drinkable at one or even two years old, but you sacrifice personality along the way.
- **Simple Beaujolais wines:** Ready from their release, about one month after the nouveau style, to about one year later.

- ✔ **Beaujolais-Villages:** Drinkable from about March of the year after the harvest until they're about two years old.
- ✔ **Lighter *cru* wines:** Drink within three years of the vintage.
- ✔ **Medium-bodied *cru* Beaujolais:** Best from one to four years after the vintage.
- ✔ **The fullest *crus*:** Drink four to seven years after the vintage, up to ten years for Moulin-à-Vent.

Chapter 4
Sparkling Champagne and Wine from Other French Regions

• •

• •

*I*s there a better-known, more popular wine in the world than Champagne? When it comes to sparkling wines, the sparkling wine we call "Champagne" has no peer. We can seriously debate what the best red wine, white wine, or dessert wine is, but it's no contest for the best sparkling wine.

The last part of this chapter gives you a taste of some of the many other wine regions in France. For lots more on these and other regions, check out the big book of *French Wine For Dummies* (published by Wiley).

What Champagne Is

Champagne is a white or rosé sparkling wine that starts its life like any other wine — as the fermented juice of grapes. But a subsequent, vital step transforms Champagne, and all the other serious sparkling wines of the world. Bottle the wine with yeast and a little sugar-wine solution, and it undergoes a *second* fermentation; this time, the bottle traps the carbon dioxide (a by-product of fermentation), so that it takes the form of tiny bubbles in the wine. Voila! You have Champagne — at least you do if this process takes place in the Champagne region of France. And that's the catch. True Champagne comes only from this one wine region. All other bubbly wines are simply "sparkling wines" — no matter what they choose to call themselves on the label.

Champagne's climate and soil

The location of the Champagne region really pushes the envelope for grape-growing: It's practically at the northernmost latitudinal limit (a little below 50 degrees latitude) in which vines can be cultivated in the northern hemisphere (see Figure 1-1).

The chalky soil of Champagne is something special. As you drive through the region, you can actually see mounds of pure white chalk. The type of soil is poor for many crops, but ideal for wine grapes, which thrive in infertile soils.

As a result of the climate and soil, the grapes that grow in the Champagne region tend to be rather tiny, but have lots of concentrated nutrients. Champagne's cool climate and its chalky, limestone soil are undoubtedly the leading factors contributing to the excellence of its sparkling wine.

The grape varieties of Champagne

Champagne is made mainly from three grape varieties:

- ✔ Pinot Noir (a red wine variety)
- ✔ Pinot Meunier (a red variety related to Pinot Noir)
- ✔ Chardonnay (a white variety)

Most Champagnes — about 85 to 90 percent of them — are a blend of about two thirds red grapes and one third Chardonnay. A few Champagnes (less than 5 percent) are 100 percent Chardonnay (they are called *blanc de blancs*); fewer yet are 100 percent red grapes (and called *blanc de noirs*). Rosé Champagnes, a small category, are usually, but not always, made from a blend of white and red grapes.

Although Champagne is primarily a white wine, the two red varieties predominate; they make up about 72 percent of the Champagne vineyards. The current percentage of planting of the three grape varieties in Champagne is 38 percent Pinot Noir, 34 percent Pinot Meunier, and 28 percent Chardonnay.

The reason that most Champagnes are blends of Pinot Noir, Pinot Meunier, and Chardonnay is that each grape variety has strengths to contribute to the final blend:

- ✔ Pinot Noir adds body, structure, aroma, and a complexity of flavors. This difficult variety likes the cool climate of the region, and it grows well in the chalky limestone soil.

- ✔ Chardonnay, a star performer in the Champagne region, gives freshness, delicacy, elegance, and finesse. For this reason, many producers make a *blanc de blancs* (Chardonnay) Champagne.

✔ Pinot Meunier contributes fruitiness, floral aromas, and a precocious character (readiness-to-drink sooner).

Styles of Champagne

Enormous variation exists among Champagnes. Some of them are sweeter than others, for example, or lighter, or more complex. We refer to the different types and tastes of Champagnes as the various *styles* of Champagnes. The spectrum of Champagne styles encompasses the following categories:

✔ Non-vintage, vintage, and prestige cuvée (premium) Champagnes

✔ Standard, *blanc de blancs, blanc de noirs,* and rosé Champagnes

✔ Brut, extra dry, and demi-sec Champagnes

✔ Light-bodied, medium-bodied, and full-bodied Champagnes

Non-vintage, vintage, and prestige cuvées

Once you understand these three styles, you can distinguish them from one another fairly easily. The challenge is that the labels don't tell you which type a Champagne is. Here is a thumb-nail description of each:

✔ **Non-vintage Champagne:** The most common type by far, these wines are blends of wines from several years, and no vintage date appears on the label; they're called "non-vintage" because they don't derive from just *one* vintage; also known as "Classic"; the least-expensive type (with a few exceptions).

✔ **Vintage Champagnes:** These are made from grapes of a single year, which is usually, but not always, a better than average year; the vintage year is on the label.

✔ **Prestige *cuvées*:** These are the producers' best Champagnes, mainly vintage Champagnes, but possibly non-vintage; the most expensive type of Champagne; Cuvée Dom Pérignon and Roederer Cristal are examples.

Blanc de blancs, blanc de noirs, and rosé Champagnes

While more than 90 percent of all Champagnes are a blend of at least two grape varieties and are white in color, three other types of Champagne exist:

✔ ***Blanc de blancs* Champagne:** *Blanc de blancs* Champagnes, made from Chardonnay only, are lighter-bodied, more acidic, and more elegant than other Champagnes. Many have vibrant, tart lemony flavors. They tend to be slightly more expensive than other Champagnes, but they also age extremely well. Some of the most famous *blanc de blancs* Champagnes are Billecart-Salmon *(bee ay car sal mohn)* Blanc de Blancs, Deutz Blanc de Blancs, and Mumm de Cramant *(crah mahn)*.

✔ ***Blanc de noirs* Champagne:** *Blanc de noirs* are the rarest type of Champagnes, especially among the larger Champagne houses. Typically golden in color, they are usually 100 percent Pinot Noir. This is the fullest-bodied type of Champagne and can accompany main courses at dinner very nicely.

✔ **Rosé Champagne:** Rosé Champagnes come in all
different hues of pink and are always *brut*
Champagnes — always dry. They get their color
from a little Pinot Noir wine that's added for that
purpose. A couple popular rosé Champagnes are
Billecart-Salmon *(sal mohn)* Brut Rosé and Gosset
(go say) Grand Rosé Brut.

From dry to sweet: Brut, Extra Dry, and Demi-Sec Champagne

Most Champagnes benefit from a *dosage (doh sahj)*, a
wine-sugar solution added as a final adjustment to the
wine after its second fermentation and aging; the
dosage balances the wine's high acidity and makes the
wine more palatable. Depending on the amount of
sugar added, and the amount of counter-balancing
acidity in the wine, you might or might not perceive the
sweetness.

Technically, six different levels of dryness are permit-
ted in Champagne but, practically speaking, we see
only three types: *Brut,* Extra Dry, and *Demi-Sec.*

Brut Champagnes

Brut Champagnes constitute the largest category of
Champagnes, but they are not a uniform category: The
only way to determine how dry or sweet a *Brut*
Champagne actually is, within the range allowed by
law, is to know the producer's style. The driest *Brut*
Champagnes are:

Bollinger	Krug
Gosset *(go say)*	Bruno Paillard
Jacquesson	Salon *(sah loan)*

Extra Dry and Demi-Sec Champagnes

Extra Dry Champagnes are "on the dry side," but somewhat sweeter than *Brut* Champagnes. This category is really marketed only in the U.S. (our national sweet tooth?). In fact, one brand, Moët & Chandon's White Star (an Extra Dry Champagne) is the best-selling Champagne in the U.S.

The only Champagne that has enough sweetness for after dinner and/or dessert is *Demi-Sec* Champagne. *Demi-Sec* Champagnes are not very common, but at least four houses (Moët & Chandon, Veuve Clicquot, Laurent-Perrier, and Louis Roederer) still make this style.

"House styles"

 We classify 25 major producers into three categories (listed alphabetically within the category) according to their house styles: light and elegant, medium-bodied, or full-bodied. The house styles of the producers are most evident in their non-vintage *Brut* (and Extra Dry) Champagnes, which they produce every year, and which make up the largest part of their production. Although producers do try to express their house styles in their vintage Champagnes, the influence of the climate in a particular vintage year can sometimes mask the house style.

Light, Elegant Style

Billecart-Salmon	Bruno Paillard
Henriot	Perrier-Jouët
Jacquesson	Piper-Heidsieck

Lanson	Pommery
Laurent-Perrier	Ruinart
G.H. Mumm	Taittinger

Medium-Bodied Style

Cattier	Moët & Chandon
Deutz	Philipponnat
Charles Heidsieck	Pol Roger

Full-Bodied Style

Bollinger	Louis Roederer
Gosset	Salon
Alfred Gratien	Veuve Clicquot Ponsardin
Krug	

Serving Champagne

 Good Champagne glasses are crucial for maximum enjoyment of your bubbly. The glass should be tall and slender, with a long stem (so that you don't hold the glass by the bowl and warm up your Champagne). A flute-shaped glass is fine for non-vintage Champagne. For vintage Champagne and prestige cuvées, we recommend a tulip-shaped glass (wider than a flute), which benefits the wine's aromas. Actually, tulip-shaped glasses (about 9 to 10 inches tall, including the stem) can be used for all Champagnes.

Serve Champagne cold (about 45° to 48° F; 7° to 9° C). Vintage Champagnes and prestige cuvées, which have more complex flavors, can be a bit warmer (50° to 53° F; 10° to 12° C). You can chill your Champagne to the desired temperature with at least four hours in the fridge, or a half hour in a tall ice bucket (with half ice and half cold water). When serving, pour the Champagne slowly into the glass so that the fizziness has time to settle down; in this way, you won't short-change your guests with a tiny pour. Fill the glass about two-thirds of the way, and refill it when just a little bit of Champagne remains in the glass; refilling restores the effervescence. Refill frequently.

After you pour your first round of Champagne, put the bottle into an ice bucket or back into the refrigerator; warm Champagne doesn't taste too good! Also, the bubbles dissipate more quickly at warmer temperatures. If you have any Champagne left over, close the bottle with a Champagne stopper and put it back into the fridge. It should keep well for two or three days.

Moving On: Southwest France

The Southwest France region mainly has a maritime (temperate) climate, influenced by the Atlantic Ocean to its west. Many of the red wines of the region are made from Cabernet Sauvignon, Cabernet Franc, and Merlot, with Malbec the main variety in Cahors. The following sections highlight the wine-making regions of Southwest France.

Bergerac

The Bergerac region makes very Bordeaux-like red wines under the Bergerac AOC designation — using all the Bordeaux varieties, especially Merlot — but without Bordeaux prices. The best Bergerac reds are barrel-aged wines from lower-yielding vineyards, and they carry the appellation Côtes de Bergerac.

Actually, almost half of Bergerac's wines are white, and a little dry rosé exists as well. The dry whites carry the AOC designation, Bergerac Sec, and derive mainly from Sémillon and Sauvignon Blanc; Muscadelle, Ondenc, and Chenin Blanc are other authorized varieties. They're similar to lighter-styled white Bordeaux wines, and are good values, often costing as little as $7 a bottle. We recommend them highly for parties, when you require a large quantity of wine — but with one caveat: They should be no more than three years old, or they won't be fresh.

Cahors

The Cahors *(cah or)* area makes red wine only; in fact, it's the most prestigious red wine district in all of Southwest France and has a wine history older than Bordeaux's. But history hasn't always been kind to Cahors. The *phylloxera* epidemic (a louse that wiped out European vineyards in the late 19th century) devastated the area to such an extent that the wine has made a comeback only in the last 40 years.

Cahors AOC wines come from the territory of 45 communes near the town of Cahors. They must derive at least 70 percent from Malbec (locally, called Auxerrois), with the remainder Tannat and/or Merlot. Two distinct styles of Cahors exist:

- ✔ The dark, tannic, traditional reds — mainly Malbec, coming from the hillsides — need about 10 years to soften, and can live for 20 or more years.

> ✔ The lighter, fruitier reds, mainly from the plains, use more Merlot and Tannat; they are drinkable within a few years of the vintage.

 Cahors wines are arguably the finest expression of the Malbec grape variety in the world. We recommend traditional producers, such as Château Lagrezette.

Béarn

The greater Béarn *(beh arn)* area, famous for Béarnaise sauce, includes the districts of Madiran and Jurançon, both individual AOC zones, as well as several anonymous wine areas. The Béarn AOC itself applies to strongly-flavored red wines as well as rosé wines deriving up to 60 percent from Tannat, along with both Cabernets and other local varieties.

Madiran

The AOC red wine district of Madiran *(mah dee rahn)* produces old-style, full-bodied, tannic reds, perfect for the hearty cuisine of the local Gascony province. The main grape in Madiran is the dark, tannic Tannat (40 to 60 percent of the blend); Cabernet Sauvignon and Cabernet Franc make up the remainder. Traditionally-made Madiran wines are certainly not wimpy and need about ten years to soften.

 Madiran has recently gained winelovers' attention thanks to the efforts of Alain Brumont of Château Montus and Château Bouscassé.

Jurançon

The Jurançon *(joo rahn sohn)* AOC district won its fame for its sweet wines, but it is the dry white, using the AOC Jurançon Sec, that dominates production today.

Both wines use the same three local varieties: Petit Manseng, Gros Manseng, and Courbu. Gros Manseng is the chief variety in the floral, intensely-flavored Jurançon Sec; Petit Manseng dominates the sweet, tangy, luscious AOC Jurançon.

Jura

Jura's most distinctive and interesting wine is Vin Jaune *(van joh'n),* the so-called "Yellow Wine." It is made from the Savagnin grape variety in all of the region's AOC districts, but is the exclusive specialty of the village (and appellation) of Château-Chalon.

Vin Jaune is comparable to a light Spanish Fino Sherry, but it's not fortified. The wine is made from late-picked, but not botrytized, Savagnin grapes. The sweet juice undergoes a slow fermentation, and then ages for a minimum of six years in old oak barrels, in cool cellars. Because the barrels are never filled to the top, a powdery film of yeasts (similar to the *flor* that forms in Fino Sherry casks) eventually develops on the wine. Because of the oxidation that results from the wine's exposure to air, and the subsequent protective character of the yeast coating, the wine has both a nuttiness and a particular tangy character. The wines are deep golden yellow or amber in color, dry, powerful, and rich in extract. And they are practically ageless. Vin Jaune comes in unique, square 620 ml bottles called *clavelins.* Unfortunately, Vin Jaune is difficult to find outside of France. But it's worth seeking out.

The Light Side: Savoie

Savoie produces some light red and rosé wine, and some decent sparkling wines, but — as you might expect in this cool, mountainous region — most of its production is crisp, dry white wine.

Savoie has one region-wide AOC (called Vin de Savoie) and three other AOCs within that appellation. What follows is a brief description of the wines in these AOC zones:

- ✔ **Vin de Savoie:** Most (about 85 percent) of the region's wines carry this general appellation, about 70 percent of which are delicate white wines. Local varieties, such as Jacquère, Roussette, Malvoisie, and Mondeuse Blanche, along with Chardonnay and Aligoté, are the dominant white varieties. Gamay, Mondeuse (a red variety called Refosco in Italy's Friuli region) and/or Pinot Noir go into the light red and rosé wines.

- ✔ **Roussette de Savoie:** A separate appellation within the Vin de Savoie AOC zone for white wines made primarily or entirely from Roussette (also known as Altesse), Savoie's best variety. If any one of four villages (Frangy, Marestel, Monteminod, or Monthoux) is appended to the Roussette de Savoie appellation, the wine must be 100 percent Roussette. Otherwise, Chardonnay can be used in making Roussette de Savoie.

- **Crépy** *(creh pee):* A small white wine AOC for vineyards along the south shore of Lake Geneva in Haute-Savoie. The grape variety for Crépy is Chasselas (often called Fendant in Switzerland's Valais area). The dry, light wines of Crépy in fact resemble Swiss wines; production is only 40,000 case a year.

- **Seyssel** *(say sell):* Perhaps Savoie's best-known appellation. The village of Seyssel is located on the banks of the Rhône River, just north of Lac du Bourget, France's largest lake. Seyssel AOC wines are dry, light whites made mainly from Roussette. Seyssel often has delicate, herbal and floral aromas, and is one of the region's best wines. Less than a third of the AOC production of Seyssel is light sparkling wine under the name Seyssel Mousseux AOC; it uses mainly Chasselas. Although much Seyssel Mousseux is consumed locally, some is exported.

 **With more than 1,400 titles to choose from, we've got a Dummies book for wherever you are in life!**